Hues of Enchantment

Golden rays stretch forth,
Touching fields of green.
Whispers of the morn,
Promise of the unseen.

Violet clouds hug dusk,
Kissing day goodnight.
Starlit dreams unfurl,
In the velvet light.

Scarlet blooms arise,
In gardens rich with cheer.
Nature sings in hues,
That only we can hear.

A river gently flows,
Reflecting skies aglow.
With every tender breeze,
Enchantment starts to grow.

In twilight's soft embrace,
The world seems to transcend.
Colors weave their magic,
As day begins to end.

The Shimmering Veil of Twilight Magic

In the hush of dusk,
Secrets softly weave.
Moonlight spills like silk,
In shadows we believe.

Stars begin to dance,
In a splendid display.
Each twinkle is a wish,
As night takes joy in play.

Whispers of the night,
Tales that float on air.
A shimmering veil,
Of dreams beyond compare.

Fog drapes o'er the hills,
Like a cloak of delight.
Enchanting hearts anew,
In the heart of the night.

With every fleeting breath,
Magic lingers near.
In the veil of twilight,
There's nothing left to fear.

Original title:
Velvet Tinctures Across the Unicorn Pane

Author: Eliora Lumiste
ISBN HARDBACK: 978-1-80562-224-6
ISBN PAPERBACK: 978-1-80563-745-5

Dreamscapes Awash in a Rainbow's Promise

In twilight's glow where dreams take flight,
A tapestry spun of colors bright.
Whispers of magic dance in the air,
Each corner of wonder beckons with care.

A river of laughter flows through the night,
As wishes take form in the silvery light.
Clouds are the castles, the stars are the keys,
Unlocking the heart with a gentle breeze.

Through fields of enchantment where shadows play,
The smiles of the moon sweep the worries away.
With creatures of fable that twirl and glide,
In this realm of dreams, we find a guide.

Each color in rainbow, a story untold,
Of bravery, friendship, of love manifold.
So step lightly now, where the dreamers convene,
In a world of delight, where all can be seen.

When dawn softly breaks and the magic takes flight,
We carry the promise of dreams through the light.
For every heart longing, a journey begins,
In the dreamscapes awash, where the adventure spins.

Ethereal Colors Against Twilight Backdrops

Dusky pinks collide,
With deep indigo skies.
A canvas of the night,
Where the imagination flies.

Emerald leaves glisten,
Bathed in twilight's glow.
Each moment is a brushstroke,
In a world we come to know.

Saffron rays entwined,
With shadows long and deep.
Ethereal whispers call,
As the world drifts to sleep.

Colors soft and bright,
As dreams begin to play.
In twilight's warm embrace,
The night steals us away.

With every blushing hue,
Stories start to bloom.
A tapestry of night,
In an ever-spreading room.

Whirlwinds of Color Amidst Fabled Tales

In the heart of the woods,
Colors swirl and twirl.
A dance of laughter sings,
In the magic of the world.

Leaves in flames of red,
Underneath a moonbeam.
Every color whispers,
A fragment of a dream.

Misty paths unfold,
With legends spun in light.
Whirlwinds of enchantment,
Drift softly through the night.

Old fairy tales linger,
In the corners of the mind.
Shadows dance like sprites,
In colors intertwined.

With each passing moment,
Fables come alive.
In whirlwinds of wonder,
Imagination thrives.

Ethereal Glows from the Whispering Woods

In twilight's grasp, the shadows sway,
A silver mist leads dreams astray.
Through ancient trees, the whispers dance,
Where starlit secrets find their chance.

The moonlight kisses ferns below,
As fireflies weave a golden glow.
Each rustling leaf, a tale retold,
Of magic past and nights of gold.

Among the roots, the fairies hum,
In shimm'ring glades, the answers come.
With every breath, the forest sighs,
In dreams, the hidden world replies.

A tapestry in twilight spun,
Where hopes and wishes freely run.
In every shadow, secrets lie,
Ethereal glows beneath the sky.

The Mystique of Colors through Time's Lens

Time dances softly, a painter bold,
With strokes of silver, crimson, gold.
Seasons shift through a prism bright,
Colors whisper secrets of day and night.

From azure skies to amber leaves,
Each hue a tale that twilight weaves.
In every shade, a memory blooms,
A path adorned with fragrant plumes.

As shadows stretch and evenings creep,
The rainbow's promise begins to sleep.
Through every moment's nuanced flair,
The soul of time is painted there.

In cerulean dreams and ruby dawns,
Existence pulses, a timeless song.
Each fleeting glance, a canvas spread,
With colors written, forever wed.

Halos of Light in a Dream Soars

In dreams, the halos softly weave,
A tapestry of night conceived.
Where starlit whispers grace the mind,
And hidden wonders wait to find.

The gentle glow of twilight's kiss,
Wraps hearts in warmth and tender bliss.
From soaring heights, the spirits glide,
With wings of light, on magic's ride.

Through realms where fantasies take flight,
The realm of dreams ignites the night.
With every breath, the colors blend,
In shimmering paths where moments bend.

Elysian views unfurling wide,
With every heartbeat, worlds collide.
An ether's glow, a dance of grace,
In dreams, we find our sacred space.

Moments of Color in the Flight of Fancy

A canvas bright on a breeze of thought,
Captures echoes of dreams unsought.
In every brushstroke, a heartbeat sways,
In moments of color, magic plays.

With cerulean whispers and vermilion sighs,
We paint our hopes across the skies.
Each fluttering leaf, a note in tune,
Moments of whimsy, beneath the moon.

In fanciful flights, where rivers gleam,
We chase the shadows of a fleeting dream.
Colors swirl in a gentle sea,
In every hue, we find the key.

Through sunsets painted with ember's grace,
We sketch our visions in time and space.
With laughter woven in every hue,
Moments of color breathe anew.

Wandering Through the Landscape of Dreams

In twilight hues where shadows blend,
I wander paths that twist and bend.
The whispers call from far away,
In dreams, I drift, where night meets day.

A golden mist, a silver stream,
Beneath the stars, I chase my dream.
Each step I take, a tale unfolds,
Of secret worlds and magic holds.

The moonlit glades, the silent glens,
Where every path through silence rends.
In fields of wishes, hearts take flight,
Adrift in hope, through endless night.

A symphony that ebbs and flows,
The gentle touch of magic glows.
I find my way through glimmering trees,
Through whispers of an ancient breeze.

The Light Beyond in Enchanted Colors

Beyond the veil of dusk's embrace,
A shimmered light begins to trace.
With pigments born from dreams anew,
It dances softly, brightens blue.

A splash of gold, a brush of green,
In every hue, enchantments glean.
The colors swirl like thoughts in flight,
Creating worlds bathed in soft light.

The laughter of stars enlivens night,
Painting the skies with pure delight.
In every shade, a story spun,
Of magic found, of battles won.

A kaleidoscope of hope and breath,
Through vibrant strands, we conquer death.
Each color tells a tale profound,
Of journeys lost, of love unbound.

Echoes Left by the Colorful Stars

In the stillness of the night,
Stars whisper softly, pure and bright.
Their echoes dance on velvet air,
A memory spun of dreams laid bare.

Each twinkle holds a secret thread,
Of wishes wished and words unsaid.
In cosmic realms, their voices sing,
Of beginnings forged and new springs.

The colors bleed from far-off lands,
Where stardust falls like gentle sands.
In silent orbs, their wisdom flows,
A gentle nudge, a spark that glows.

When night descends and shadows creep,
These stars remind, they will not sleep.
Their whispers, vibrant, full of grace,
In every heart, they find a place.

Celestial Ribbons and Tints of Hope

In the twilight's tender fold,
Celestial ribbons twist and hold.
With hints of lavender and rose,
They weave a tale that gently flows.

A tapestry of dreams unfurl,
Each thread a wish from yonder world.
With every shimmer, fears abate,
Illuminating hope, a fateful gate.

The winds of change swirl ever near,
Caressing souls, dispelling fear.
Through every hue, a promise thrives,
In every heart, the dream arrives.

So lift your gaze to skies above,
Embrace the light, the warmth of love.
For though the night may seem so deep,
These ribbons guide, their secrets keep.

Glimmering Shades in the Fabric of Myth

In twilight's embrace, legends unfold,
Where shadows and whispers weave tales bold.
Each stitch of the night, a story to tell,
In the tapestry woven where dreamers dwell.

Elusive are visions that dance in the air,
With glimmering shades that enchant and ensnare.
From echoes of magic, the past does awake,
In the fabric of myth, our hearts start to quake.

The flicker of starlight upon silver streams,
Unravel the threads of forgotten dreams.
In the loom of the cosmos, we seek and we find,
A glimpse of the stories long left behind.

So gather your courage, let wonder ignite,
As glimmering shades guide you through the night.
With each step you take, let the magic align,
In the fabric of myth, your fate will entwine.

Charmed Light Enveloping the Dreamscape

Through the velvet dusk, a soft glow begins,
A charmed light weaving where silence spins.
In shadows, it dances, a flicker so shy,
As dreams start to shimmer and gently fly.

The night whispers secrets that only we share,
With each breath of magic, we float through the air.
Enveloped in warmth, like a lover's embrace,
We wander the dreamscape, a luminous space.

Stars twinkle softly, a guiding refrain,
In the heart of the night, where wishes are lain.
A symphony hums under moonlight's allure,
In this charmed light, our spirits are pure.

With visions unfolding like petals in bloom,
The dreamscape surrounds, dispelling the gloom.
So linger a while in this wonderous glow,
For the magic of dreams is the truth we all know.

A Journey Through the Hues of Enchantment

Upon the horizon, the dawn starts to sway,
A journey unfolds through the hues of the day.
With colors ablaze, like a painter's delight,
We move through the canvas of morning light.

With each careful step, the palette expands,
In whispers of wonder, the universe stands.
From cobalt to saffron, the spectrum ignites,
Inviting our spirits to dance in the sights.

Through valleys and peaks, where the wildflowers grow,
The hues of enchantment begin to bestow.
Moments of magic in every embrace,
A journey through colors, a tender trace.

With laughter and light, let the adventure flow,
In the symphony of life, where enchantments grow.
So take to the sky, let your heart soar and sing,
For this journey through hues, like a dream, will take
wing.

Crystalline Echoes in Celestial Waters

In rippling silence, reflections arise,
Crystalline echoes beneath watchful skies.
The waters, a mirror, reveal depths untold,
Where stories of starlight and wishes unfold.

Each drop tells a tale of the cosmos at play,
In celestial waters where night meets the day.
The whispers of galaxies, soft as a sigh,
Invite us to dance in the vastness of high.

With every soft shimmer, a heartbeat we feel,
In the realms of the magic, the mystical heal.
As we gaze into waters that shimmer and flow,
Crystalline echoes guide us where we should go.

So listen to secrets that linger and bloom,
In the still of the night, let destiny loom.
For in these celestial waters we find,
A connection to wonders that twine with the mind.

The Enigmatic Glow of Fantastical Lands

In twilight's grasp, where shadows breathe,
A whisper stirs the ancient trees,
With secrets held in mystic sighs,
As dreams awaken, gently rise.

The nightingale sings of moonlit quests,
Where fairies dance in silken vests,
Through hidden paths of emerald bright,
They weave the threads of purest light.

The rivers hum their timeless lore,
With silver scales, they kiss the shore,
While twilight weaves its velvet veil,
In every heart, a wondrous tale.

And here, in lands both wide and far,
We chase the glow of every star,
Embracing magic, boundless, free,
In enigmatic harmony.

So venture forth, in dreams take flight,
Where every heart can seek the light,
For in these lands of joy and strife,
Awaits the true enchanted life.

Painting the Mists with Unseen Colors

In dawn's embrace, a canvas lies,
A tapestry of soft sunrise,
With whispers held in swirling hue,
The mists unveil a world anew.

Brushstrokes dance upon the waves,
Where gentle winds, like spirits, braves,
Colors blend in sweet delight,
Transforming day from starry night.

With strokes of gold and shades of blue,
The painter's heart breathes magic true,
As each misted hue finds its song,
In harmony where we belong.

Through twisted paths of fog and blush,
In every heartbeat, feel the rush,
For unseen colors spark the mind,
In this great dance, our souls aligned.

So let the mists come paint the day,
With vibrant dreams to light the way,
In every glance, a story swells,
A journey held in joyful spells.

Aquamarine Waters and Fiery Skies

The sun dips low in fiery grace,
As evening waves caress the place,
Aquamarine, the water's gleam,
Reflects the sky, a vivid dream.

With ardent hearts, we cast our lines,
In search of treasures, fate aligns,
While glowing embers mark our trail,
As nature sings, the night will hail.

The stars arise, like crystals bright,
A celestial feast in velvet night,
Where fish and flame entwine in dance,
A timeless waltz of fate and chance.

Beneath the waves, the mystics roam,
In depths of azure, they find home,
While skies ablaze with fiery tongues,
Erasing shadows where hope clings.

So let us brave the tide and swell,
With every wave, our hearts will tell,
Of aquamarine waters' embrace,
And the fiery skies that grant us grace.

Celestial Petals in the Eternal Garden

In gardens vast, where wonders bloom,
Celestial petals fill the room,
A fragrance sweet, a dance of light,
In eternal whispers, day and night.

With every step, the blossoms sway,
In shades of dusk and golden ray,
Fleeting moments touch the ground,
In radiant circles, joy is found.

The stars above join in our cheer,
Each twinkling light a memory dear,
For time stands still in sacred space,
Within this garden's warm embrace.

As petals drift on morning air,
They carry secrets beyond compare,
Inviting hearts to pause and dream,
In magic's grasp, all things redeem.

So wander deep where wonders twine,
With every breath, the stars align,
In this eternal garden's glow,
Our spirits soar, their love shall flow.

Shimmering Paths of Celestial Journeys

Beneath the stars, where whispers weave,
The shimmering paths that dreams believe.
Moonlit echoes call the brave,
Through twilight realms, our souls will rave.

With every step on cosmic sand,
Adventures bloom, both wild and grand.
Time unravels in glistening streams,
Fulfilling softly our deepest dreams.

Waves of stardust, dance and play,
Guiding hearts along the way.
In the silence, magic sings,
As we embrace what starlight brings.

Journey forth, the compass shines,
Infinity within the lines.
Together we shall seek and find,
A universe that's intertwined.

A Palette of Legends Under Cosmic Canopies

Underneath the cosmic dome,
Legends whisper, calling home.
Colors blend in twilight skies,
As starlit dreams begin to rise.

Each shadow holds a tale unique,
In stillness, past and future speak.
The palette dipped in midnight grace,
Brushes strokes of time and space.

Captured hues of heart's delight,
In the dance of day and night.
Echoes of the past resonate,
With brush and quill, we create fate.

With every hue, a story spun,
Of battles fought and victories won.
Beneath the cosmic canopies,
We find ourselves in whispered pleas.

Celestial Blooms in a Glimmering Dawn

At dawn's embrace, the stars retreat,
Celestial blooms rise to greet.
Petals unfurl in golden light,
A symphony of day breaks night.

In gardens rich with dreams anew,
The whispers of the heavens brew.
With every breath, the universe hums,
Creating magic as morning comes.

Sunbeams dance on soft, dewy leaves,
In this harmony, the spirit believes.
Nature's canvas, pure and bright,
Paints our hopes in colors of light.

Together we bloom, hearts intertwined,
In this glimmering dawn so defined.
With each heartbeat, a new refrain,
Celestial echoes through joy and pain.

The Alchemy of Light and Shadow

In twilight's weave, where shadows play,
The alchemy of night and day.
With every flicker, stories blend,
The light and shadow meet, transcend.

Secrets lie in dusk's embrace,
Where dreams and fears find tender space.
Moonbeams dance with flickering flame,
In this realm, nothing is the same.

Alchemy turns the dull to bright,
Creating wonders in soft moonlight.
Together they speak, a silent song,
Guiding the lost, where they belong.

Within this tapestry, we find,
A balance forged, each thread aligned.
The alchemy of light and shade,
In every heart, a promise laid.

Chromatic Visions in the Fairyland Waters

In waters bright where color sways,
A dance of light in twilight plays.
Reflections twist on liquid dreams,
Painting worlds in soft moonbeams.

Whispers rise from depths unknown,
Each ripple tells a tale once sown.
Glimmers of gold and sapphire tones,
Echo softly in ancient stones.

With every splash, a secret shared,
Mysteries linger, spirits bared.
The fairies flit on rainbow streams,
Their laughter drifts like simmering creams.

Beneath the arch of starlit skies,
The tapestry of life just lies.
Woven threads of crimson and jade,
Craft a realm where dreams are laid.

So come and sip the colors pure,
Embrace the magic, feel the allure.
In fairyland where wonders flow,
Let the chromatic river glow.

Luminous Echoes of Ethereal Realities

In twilight realms where shadows glide,
Echoes dance on a dreamy tide.
Whispers of light in colors bold,
Unravel stories of ages told.

The stars knit tales in threads of gold,
Murmurs of myths both new and old.
Cosmic songs weave through the night,
Luminous beams in radiant flight.

Each heartbeat sings in hues divine,
Gathering visions in sacred line.
Harmonies swirl like gentle streams,
A symphony of vibrant dreams.

Through veils of mist, the echoes rise,
Carrying secrets from starry skies.
Illuminated paths we tread,
With every thought, more light is spread.

In ethereal realms where wonders sway,
Find solace in the shimmering play.
For every shadow, a beam of grace,
Luminous echoes in this sacred space.

Fantasia of Hues in Celestial Gardens

In gardens vast where colors bloom,
Life unfurls with fragrance sweet as loom.
Petals whisper tales of light,
Fantasia born of sheer delight.

The sun spills gold on emerald leaves,
A painter, weaving what heart believes.
Each flower's blush a story spun,
Tales of love beneath the sun.

Iridescent butterflies drift by,
Spreading magic as they flutter high.
In every sigh, a dream takes flight,
A dance of colors in purest light.

The stars peek out when day concedes,
Bathing blooms in evening's beads.
Celestial secrets softly throng,
In gardens where the heart belongs.

Through every breeze, a melody lives,
A canvas where the spirit gives.
In hues of joy, let hearts be free,
In celestial gardens, we find glee.

Harmonics of Color in the Essence of Daydreams

In the canvas of the mind's delight,
Color harmonies take to flight.
Daydreams dance on silk-edged skies,
Painting worlds where wonder lies.

With strokes of blue and glints of gold,
Stories of magic find their hold.
Whispers of lavender gently sway,
As fantasies weave through sunlit play.

In every hue, a tale unfolds,
Mysteries whispered, secrets told.
Crimson laughter, emerald sighs,
Echo through where passion flies.

With each heartbeat, colors blend,
A kaleidoscope that has no end.
In the essence where dreams take shape,
Life's vibrant tapestry we escape.

Beyond the veil where visions gleam,
In the depths of an endless dream.
With harmonics bright, let spirits soar,
In color's embrace, forevermore.

Secrets of Color in the Whispering Breeze

In twilight's hush, the colors sigh,
A palette painted in the sky.
Whispers of lavender drift in the air,
Secrets of nature, tender and rare.

Emerald leaves in the softest light,
Glimmer like jewels in the night.
Crimson shadows flicker and fade,
Echoes of dreams in the glade.

Golden rays tease the morning dew,
An artist's brush—brilliant and true.
Serenade of colors, a gentle embrace,
Fields alive with a vibrant grace.

The breeze carries tales of the past,
In hues that are woven and vast.
Cerulean skies call the heart to soar,
In this world, we yearn for more.

Petals of joy underfoot do lay,
Whispers of color lead us astray.
In every corner, a story unfolds,
Nature's secrets in colors bold.

Tints of Wonder Beneath Celestial Canopies

Stars twinkle softly, a cosmic show,
Painting the heavens with delicate glow.
A tapestry woven in midnight hues,
Whispers of magic in maroon and blues.

Beneath the canopy of dreams untold,
Silver threads shimmer like strands of gold.
Each twinkle a secret, each glimmer a song,
Guiding our spirits where we belong.

Crimson clouds brush the horizon's edge,
As night unfurls her velvet pledge.
Lunar embers dance on a gentle sea,
Tints of wonder, wild and free.

The auroras unfurl in a mystic ballet,
Casting shadows that whisper and sway.
Colorful secrets of ancient lore,
Spill from the cosmos to our very core.

In the hush of night, listen and dream,
Where stardust twinkles and wishes gleam.
Beneath celestial canopies, we find our way,
Awash in wonder, night turns to day.

The Wild Dance of Color on Mythic Wings

In forests deep where silence weaves,
Creatures of color flutter like leaves.
Their wings ablaze with a vibrant dance,
In shadows broken, they spin and prance.

With every flicker, a tale is spun,
Magic unfurls with the rising sun.
Golds and greens in a radiant twirl,
The wild dance beckons, a fanciful whirl.

Through fragrant blooms, they rise and dive,
In this world of color, they come alive.
Cerulean skies are their endless stage,
Each flutter a note on a bold new page.

From emerald glades to sapphire streams,
They weave a tapestry of vivid dreams.
In whispers of color, their spirits soar,
On mythic wings, forever explore.

As dusk descends, the colors fade,
Yet in our hearts, their magic is laid.
For in each flutter, we glimpse the light,
The wild dance of color ignites the night.

Beneath the moon's gaze, they softly glide,
A symphony of hues, a wondrous ride.
On mythic wings, they challenge the day,
A reminder that color will never sway.

Dappled Dreams Beneath the Realm of Stars

In the hush of twilight, shadows play,
Dappled dreams dance at the close of day.
Among the stars, wishes take flight,
Glittering softly in the velvety night.

Nature's brush strokes paint the scene,
In hues of hope, where we have been.
Flecks of silver in the cool evening air,
Whispers of magic hang everywhere.

Rays of moonlight stream like cascading streams,
Illuminating valleys that cradle our dreams.
The world is alive with enchanting hues,
Each shadow and shimmer, a secret muse.

With every star that twinkles above,
Comes a reminder of beauty and love.
Dappled dreams whisper tales yet spun,
In the heart of the night, we become one.

As dawn creeps in with a tender sigh,
Colors awaken in the morning sky.
Yet beneath the realm of starlit scenes,
Dappled dreams linger in soft moonbeams.

So find the magic in every glance,
In every sunset, in every chance.
For in the night sky, secrets gleam,
Dappled dreams twinkle, forever a theme.

Mystical Waters and Their Vibrant Reflections

Beneath the willow's gentle sway,
A lake of dreams begins to play.
Whispers dance upon the breeze,
As shadows mingle with the trees.

Mirrors gleam in the twilight glow,
Where secrets of the night do flow.
Each ripple speaks in softest tones,
Of ancient tales and timeless bones.

Lanterns flicker, stars in sight,
Greeting the deepening night.
The moon drapes silver on the hue,
Of vibrant waters, ever true.

Fishes dart with gleeful grace,
Chasing dreams in this hidden place.
Nature hums a soothing song,
Where every heart and soul belong.

In stillness, magic takes its stand,
A painter's brush in nature's hand.
The vibrant reflections weave anew,
A tapestry of midnight blue.

Tapestry of Colorful Whimsy

In gardens where the wild things grow,
The blooms, like laughter, start to flow.
Petals painted, bright and bold,
A vibrant story yet untold.

Winds whisper secrets at the gate,
Of colors that will not abate.
A bath of sun, a splash of rain,
Transforms the world in a sweet refrain.

Bees amble through their busy dance,
Each flower framing nature's chance.
The sky above in gilded hue,
A canvas stretched, forever new.

Ladybugs dot the tapestry,
Painting joy where none can flee.
In every nook, a sparkle stays,
Creating magic in the rays.

So let the heart be light and free,
In this colorful tapestry.
With each new shade, life takes its flight,
A joyful swirl of pure delight.

Enchanted Rainbows in Twilight's Embrace

As twilight falls, the colors blend,
A rainbow's arc begins to send.
Brushstrokes of magic form and fade,
In a softly woven serenade.

Clouds cradle hues of pink and gold,
Whispers of silver tales retold.
Stars twinkle in the boundless ink,
Where dreams alight, and spirits think.

The horizon dances, vibrant sway,
Unfurling wonders at the end of day.
Nature stirs in twilight's grace,
Embracing night in soft embrace.

From emerald hills to sapphire skies,
Each pigment draws away our sighs.
A moment caught in stillness, bright,
Where colors merge, igniting light.

So take a breath, let your heart fly,
Underneath this vast, enchanted sky.
In every shade, we find a spark,
Guiding us home through the velvet dark.

Fantasia of Colors on Gossamer Wings

In gardens where the fairies dwell,
A fantasia begins to swell.
With gossamer wings, they dance and play,
In brilliant hues that chase the gray.

Each flutter brings a tale untold,
Of wonders bright and hearts of gold.
Petals shimmer in the sunlight's kiss,
A moment woven pure bliss.

Beneath the boughs of ancient trees,
Whispers drift upon the breeze.
A splash of amber, a stroke of blue,
The vibrant dreamscape beckons you.

From dawn till dusk, the colors glide,
An endless journey, side by side.
A palette born from love's embrace,
Painting joy in every space.

So let your spirit rise and soar,
On wings of color, evermore.
In this fantasia, we shall find,
The beauty of our hearts entwined.

Silken Echoes of Fantastical Dreams

In gardens where the shadows play,
Whispers of magic drift and sway.
Each petal tells a tale untold,
Of secrets wrapped in threads of gold.

Through twilight's veil, the stars emerge,
With silver hopes that softly surge.
They twinkle in a dance so bright,
Guiding souls through the endless night.

The moonlight weaves a gentle sound,
Of dreams where lost companions found.
With every echo, hearts will soar,
In realms of wonder evermore.

A tapestry of gleaming light,
Enfolds the world in soft delight.
Where every sigh and laugh still gleams,
In silken echoes of fantastical dreams.

The Prism's Heart Beneath Starlit Skies

Underneath the velvet night,
A prism glows with colors bright.
Each hue a wish, a fleeting sigh,
Dances softly in the sky.

The heartbeat of the stars above,
Is woven through with whispered love.
In every shade a story weaves,
Of hidden paths and secret leaves.

The canvas spreads, a wondrous sight,
As shadows dip and colors fight.
Through every hue, a tale unfolds,
In whispers soft, the heart beholds.

And in this glow, the night will share,
The dreams that linger in the air.
Beneath the stars, each soul will find,
The prism's heart, forever kind.

Threads of Color Woven in Myth

In ancient looms, the stories spin,
Threads of color, where dreams begin.
Each strand a legacy of lore,
Binding the past to evermore.

With twilight's brush, the tales are drawn,
As daylight fades to dusky dawn.
In every weave, a spirit sings,
Of heroes bold and wondrous things.

The fables twist like vines that grow,
Immerse us deep in softening glow.
Through every knot, new worlds arise,
With sparkling hope that never dies.

In shadows deep, the magic glows,
Where ancient wisdom gently shows.
Threads of color intertwined,
In a fabric of myth, we find.

Chromatic Fantasies on Moonlit Shores

Upon the waves, the moonlight plays,
As chromatic dreams in silver rays.
The ocean hums a mystic tune,
Beneath the watchful, glowing moon.

Each tide brings forth a story new,
Of adventures wrapped in ocean's hue.
Stars reflect in gentle waves,
Whispers of the journeys brave.

With every splash, a world ignites,
Dancing beneath the starry lights.
A canvas vast, where spirits soar,
In chromatic fantasies by the shore.

In laughter sweet, and shadows long,
The night unfolds a haunting song.
Through rhythms of the sea and sand,
We lose ourselves, hand in hand.

Ethereal Resonance of the Sacred Spectrum

In twilight hues where shadows blend,
The colors dance, their whispers send.
With every note, a spirit's sigh,
A symphony where dreams comply.

Gentle echoes through the air,
A call to souls, both bold and rare.
They weave a song through night's embrace,
As starlit chords begin to trace.

The rainbow bends through ancient trees,
Where laughter mingles with the breeze.
Each cherished tone, a memory forged,
In every heart, the magic surged.

With vibrant rays, the shadows flee,
As love's pure light sets spirits free.
An ethereal realm, so close yet far,
Guides lost hearts beneath a star.

To dance in realms where colors gleam,
Is to awaken from a dream.
In sacred echoes, they embrace,
The harmony of time and space.

Luminescent Whispers from the Otherworld

From depths unknown, the whispers rise,
Like silken threads beneath the skies.
A gentle beckon, soft and pure,
Entwined in light, they softly lure.

Through hidden paths where shadows wane,
Their luminescence guides the way.
Each flicker tells of tales untold,
In ancient dreams, their truths unfold.

They shimmer bright, with secrets shared,
Offering solace, all souls dared.
Brushed by the light of other times,
In harmony with magic rhymes.

The moonlight weaves a tender crest,
Where hearts unite and spirits rest.
In whispered tones, the night enthralls,
As endless echoes softly call.

A gentle glide through realms unknown,
With every breath, the seeds are sown.
From luminous whispers, strength we claim,
In the otherworld, we find our name.

Spectrum of Secrets in Dreamer's Grove

In Dreamer's Grove where wishes bloom,
A spectrum glows that chases gloom.
The secrets held in nature's care,
Bring forth the magic of the air.

In hidden glades, the colors pulse,
A gentle wave, inviting us.
With every rustle, life awakes,
The heart of dreams that never breaks.

A tangle of hues, both bright and stark,
Whispering truths that light the dark.
In every shade, enchantment thrives,
Where every thought and feeling strives.

Through petals soft, the visions flow,
In harmony, the spirits glow.
For in this grove, all doubts will cease,
As every heart discovers peace.

A tapestry of dreams unspools,
In sacred bounds where nature rules.
The spectrum gleams, revealing fate,
In Dreamer's Grove, we celebrate.

Harmonics of Light in Fairyland's Heart

In Fairyland where laughter rings,
The light creates its own fine strings.
Each note a spark that lifts the soul,
In joyful chorus, we are whole.

The vibrant hues of dusk unite,
With every pulse, the stars ignite.
In every breath, a magic share,
In harmonics, we find our care.

The fairies dance on beams of gold,
Their stories in the light unfold.
With every twirl, they weave a tale,
Of endless dreams in twilight's veil.

Underneath a canopy bright,
The world awakens with delight.
Each twinkle, like a secret glance,
Inviting us to join the dance.

In Fairyland, the light confides,
In joys where every heart abides.
A radiant glow, a realm of art,
In harmonics, we find our heart.

Radiant Dreams in a Prism of Light

In twilight's hush, the shadows play,
Colors swirl in the fading day.
Whispers of hope in the evening breeze,
Embrace the magic that never flees.

Glimmers of gold on the horizon's face,
Every moment a new, enchanted space.
With every heartbeat, the dreams take flight,
Radiant wonders come alive in the night.

Stars like diamonds in the deep, dark sky,
Dancing softly as wishes fly.
Looking closely, you'll find the gleam,
Life is woven from a vibrant dream.

Each echoing laugh, a spark of delight,
Illuminates paths in the soft twilight.
Feel the warmth of the dreams you chase,
In the prism of light, find your place.

So gather your hopes, let them ignite,
For in every heart lies a radiant light.
Chasing the colors that brightly gleam,
You'll find your truth in a universe of dream.

Gossamer Threads Woven with Stardust

In the stillness of night, a tale unfolds,
Of gossamer dreams and secrets untold.
Threads of starlight in the cosmic loom,
Gentle whispers weave through the gloom.

A tapestry woven with love and care,
Twinkling moments scattered everywhere.
Each sparkle a promise, each thread a song,
In the dance of time, we all belong.

Hold tightly to hopes as they shimmer bright,
Guided by wishes on a celestial flight.
Every heartbeat echoes, a story to say,
In the fabric of night, we find our way.

With every breath, the universe sighs,
Woven with magic beneath endless skies.
Among the stars, let your spirit soar,
For deep in your heart, lies a cosmic lore.

So follow the paths where the starlight bends,
Embrace the threads where the cosmos blends.
In the gentle embrace of dreams aligned,
You'll find the stardust, your heart entwined.

Unveiling Secrets in the Aurora's Glow

Beneath the northern lights, a secret scheme,
Whispers of magic ignite the dream.
Colors cascade in a flowing embrace,
Painting the night with elegance and grace.

Each hue reveals what the heart conceals,
In the dance of shadows, the truth reveals.
Soft winds carry tales through the frosty air,
Moments of wonder suspended with care.

The aurora sings in a symphonic light,
A melody echoing through the night.
With every shimmer, the stories unfold,
The warmth of the secrets in colors bold.

Under the blanket of a starry dome,
Find the whispers that lead you home.
In the glow of the night, let worries cease,
Embrace the magic, and discover peace.

So lift your gaze, let your spirit flow,
In the secrets unveiled by the aurora's glow.
For in this dance of light and shade,
Lies the heart of the dreams that never fade.

The Dance of Shades in a Celestial Realm

In a celestial realm where shadows waltz,
Figures entwined, without a fault.
Mysteries linger in the twilight shade,
Quietly whispering choices made.

The stars are companions in this ballet,
Guiding gentle spirits along the way.
Every twirl holds a glimpse of light,
In the dance of shadows, hearts take flight.

Whirls of calm, as the night draws near,
Unseen magic flutters, crystal clear.
In the hush of the cosmos, let time dissolve,
Discover the rhythms in which we evolve.

Each movement a promise, each pause a prayer,
Celestial blessings hanging in the air.
With each beaten path, the shadows gleam,
In the heart of the night, realize the dream.

So twirl with the shades in this endless space,
Embrace the journey; find your place.
In the dance of the stars, let your spirit soar,
For in the celestial realm, we are evermore.

The Alchemy of Colors in the Dreamweaver's Hands

In twilight's grasp, hues softly blend,
Dreamweaver spins, as shadows send.
With whispers of gold, and midnight deep,
Awakening worlds where secrets seep.

A canvas adorned with a spectral flight,
Each stroke ignites the eternal night.
Crimson rivers and azure skies,
Where reality fades, and magic lies.

With fingers dancing, the palette sings,
Emerald leaves, as the sunrise brings.
Hearts painted warm in the pastel glow,
Guiding the lost where wonders flow.

Every shade holds a tale untold,
Whispered by spirits both young and old.
In the dreamer's hands, the colors weave,
A tapestry rich for those who believe.

And as the night embraces the day,
The alchemy churns, come what may.
For in visions bright, and shadows cast,
The harmony of hues will ever last.

Serendipity of Tints in a Magical Forest

In the heart of woods where wonders bloom,
A dance of colors dispels the gloom.
Rustling leaves in a playful tease,
Crafting stories upon the breeze.

Golden sunbeams filter through,
Painting dreams in every hue.
Lilac whispers and sapphire streams,
Here, reality mingles with dreams.

Misty mornings in emerald embrace,
Each shade a step through a timeless space.
Serendipity whispers at every turn,
Inviting hearts that long to learn.

Crimson blossoms in secret glades,
Echoing laughter as twilight fades.
A symphony hums through branches high,
Where colors waltz beneath the sky.

In shadows deep where moonlight glows,
The forest unfurls its cherished throes.
A magical realm, forever free,
In every tint, a fantasy.

Fragments of Light in Otherworldly Vistas

In realms unseen where starlight bends,
Fragments of light weave and wend.
Galaxies twinkling in whispered tones,
Echoes of secrets made of stones.

Rivers of luminescence flow,
Painting dreams in a cosmic glow.
Each twinkle a brushstroke, bold and bright,
A dance of colors, lost to night.

Beyond horizons in twilight's cage,
Where colors shimmer, freed from age.
Every heartbeat a radiant stream,
In otherworldly vistas they gleam.

Translucent shades on ethereal wings,
With melodies sung by celestial things.
The universe whispers, a vibrant call,
In fragments of light, we find it all.

And as time weaves through ribbons of space,
We chase the light in a tender embrace.
For in every particle, we come to find,
The magic of colors, eternally entwined.

A Symphony of Colors in Realm Unseen

In a realm of dreams, where colors play,
A symphony blooms at the break of day.
Each shade a note in a grand design,
A melody woven in threads divine.

Violet whispers blend with emerald hues,
Every laugh dances on morning dews.
From golden rays to the silver night,
Harmony sparkles with pure delight.

Circles of light on the softest air,
A tapestry spun with exquisite care.
As shadows shift and the spirits sway,
In this unseen realm, we drift away.

The pitter-patter of rain in bloom,
Each drop a color that banishes gloom.
In vivid strokes, the story flows,
A canvas alive where imagination grows.

A dance of hues, both gentle and bold,
In the silence, the vibrant unfolds.
With every heartbeat, the colors blend,
In this symphony, our spirits mend.

Flickers of Enchantment in Glistening Night

In twilight's embrace, where whispers reside,
The stars weave their tales, a tapestry wide.
Moonlight ignites with a silvery spark,
A dance of the dreams, in the heart of the dark.

Ghostly shadows sway, in a delicate trance,
Mysterious fairies twirl in their dance.
The air crackles bright with enchanted delight,
As secrets unfold in the still of the night.

Gentle winds carry soft echoes of cheer,
Laughter of nymphs that only we hear.
Time stands suspended, the world feels anew,
In flickers of magic, where wishes come true.

A glimmering path through the dim forest weaves,
With petals like jewels and sighs from the leaves.
Each step a reminder of wonders untold,
In dreams and in stories, new and old.

So linger awhile, let your spirit take flight,
In flickers of enchantment, all bathed in light.

The Radiance of Dreams Awash in Shadows

Beneath the thick canopy of stars so bright,
Dreams weave their magic like threads of pure light.
In silence they shimmer, shy yet so bold,
Whispers of wishes in night's gentle fold.

The moon's silver glance shines on slumbering dreams,
Caught in the dance of soft, silver beams.
The shadows embrace what the heart longs to find,
In the glow of the night, possibilities unwind.

With laughter like raindrops that fall from above,
The echoes of hope twine with unspoken love.
These moments of beauty, elusive yet near,
Illuminate paths that flicker and clear.

So close your bright eyes, let the visions take flight,
The radiance of dreams, a magical sight.
For within every shadow, a secret awaits,
To guide us through portals, to ancient gates.

Awash in these wonders, the night softly hums,
Telling of journeys and what truly comes.
Each gleam a reminder to believe and to hold,
The radiant stories that forever unfold.

Silken Tides and Celestial Reflections

In the hush of the dusk, where the ocean sighs,
Silken tides rise up to caress cloudy skies.
The stars dip in waters that glimmer like glass,
Reflected emotions, as moments all pass.

The moon drapes its silver on waves that embrace,
Ripples of secrets unveiled in their grace.
Awash in the twilight, the world seems to blend,
A fusion of longing that time cannot end.

Deep echoes of dreams whisper soft through the night,
Guiding lost hearts with a shimmering light.
Celestial beings on soft breezes glide,
While love flows like currents, with nothing to hide.

So drift with the whispers, let go of your fears,
As tides carry wishes, dissolving our tears.
In silken waves, where all sorrows take flight,
We dance with the cosmos, in pure, sweet delight.

A tapestry woven of hope's warm embrace,
In shadows and light, we find our true place.
Celestial reflections call gently to me,
To join in the harmony, wild and free.

Brushstrokes of Magic in Dappled Light

In glades where the sunlight paints patterns divine,
Brushstrokes of magic in every align.
Leafy canopies filter the golden hue,
Creating a canvas where wonders ensue.

The air is alive with a painter's soft sigh,
As butterflies dance and the wildflowers fly.
Each moment a stroke, rich in vibrant delight,
In dappled, sweet spaces, the heart takes to flight.

A flick of the wand, as the shadows entwine,
Dreams come alive in a world so benign.
Laughter resounds, like a sweet serenade,
In realms where the mundane is carefully made.

So wander through whispers of light and of shade,
Embrace the enchantment that nature has played.
For each brushstroke reveals a new path, untold,
In the dappled light's warmth, let your spirit unfold.

In this dance of the day, where the sun meets the trees,
We capture the magic, as easy as breeze.
In brushstrokes of wonder, we find our true might,
In the heart of the forest, all bathed in light.

Whispers of the Enchanted Veil

In twilight's embrace, the secrets stir,
A dance of shadows, the light a blur.
Ancient tales in the wind, they weave,
Promises linger for those who believe.

Through silver leaves, the whispers call,
In hidden glens where the twilight falls.
Echoes of laughter, a soft refrain,
Entwined with the mist, like a gentle chain.

Mysteries cradle in the moon's embrace,
Time drifts slowly in this sacred space.
With every heartbeat, the magic flows,
Unraveling stories the night bestows.

Beneath the stars, where wishes bloom,
The air is fragrant with sweet perfume.
Swaying under the pendulum of night,
Dreamers find solace in the muted light.

Hand in hand with the shadows we roam,
Each step an echo of stories unknown.
In this enchanted veil, hearts will unite,
With whispers of hope wrapping us tight.

Luminous Shadows in Celestial Gardens

In gardens where stars adore the night,
Luminous blooms gleam with cosmic light.
Petals whisper secrets to the sky,
While moonbeams dance, inviting dreams to fly.

Through fragrant paths where the stardust plays,
A melody weaves through the shimmering rays.
Night's gentle brush paints a vivid scene,
Crafting a tapestry of worlds unseen.

Glistening echoes of laughter resound,
In the heart of the garden, magic is found.
Crickets serenade the velvet air,
Each note a wish, a promise to share.

When shadows whisper, they spin a tale,
Of ethereal realms where hopes never pale.
With every heartbeat, the cosmos embrace,
Luring us into this captivating space.

Awash in the glow of celestial spree,
We wander the paths of infinity.
In luminous gardens, our spirits soar,
Finding forever in the cosmic lore.

Gossamer Hues of Dreaming Night

Upon the canvas of a sky so deep,
Gossamer hues in silence creep.
Twinkling lanterns in the velvet flow,
Guide the dreamers where the starlit glow.

Winds carry whispers of tales untold,
In shadows' embrace where dreams unfold.
Each shimmer a heartbeat, a tender sigh,
Of wishes fermenting in the night sky.

Beneath the tapestry where fantasies lie,
Colors blend softly, like lullabies.
A symphony of starlight, soft and bright,
Wraps every heart in the folds of the night.

In the cradle of hours, time holds its breath,
Each moment rich with a quiet depth.
Dancing through vistas of velvet and gold,
We chase the dreams that have yet to unfold.

Gossamer hues in a world so new,
Awakening magic in every hue.
For in the night where the wild hearts tread,
Lies the promise of dreams, softly spread.

Chasing Spectrum in Ethereal Realms

In realms where colors endlessly collide,
Chasing spectral wonders, we glide.
Radiant rainbows, a vivid delight,
Illuminate pathways in the silence of night.

Through whispers of twilight, we wander free,
Where shadows stretch into infinity.
Each hue a journey, a tale to unfold,
In ethereal realms, for the daring and bold.

As twilight beckons with its gentle hand,
We chase the spectrum through dream's vast land.
Galaxies twirl in the tapestry bright,
Crafting illusions within our sight.

Every heartbeat syncs with the colors' song,
Echoing truths where we all belong.
Painted with stardust, our spirits ignite,
In luminous realms, dancing in light.

With laughter that sparkles like dew in the morn,
We find ourselves endlessly reborn.
Chasing the spectrum in a world so grand,
Creating magic as we reach for each strand.

Mystical Shades Beneath the Moon's Embrace

In shadows deep where secrets dwell,
The moonlight weaves a silver spell.
With whispers soft, the night unfolds,
Enchanting tales that time retolds.

Beneath the beams, the willows sway,
In moonlit dreams, the world drifts away.
Each glimmering spark, a story spun,
A dance of shadows 'til night is done.

The owl takes flight, a silent quest,
While starlit paths choose hearts to test.
In every rustle, in every sigh,
The magic breathes, as night draws nigh.

The woodlands hum with ancient lore,
Where secrets linger, forevermore.
The brook, it laughs, in silver streams,
Carrying wishes and midnight dreams.

So take a step beneath the sheen,
Embrace the night, let magic glean.
For in the dark, the wonders gleam,
And life is but a moonlit dream.

Chasing Rainbows in the Cosmic Ether

In skies where colors merge and blend,
A fleeting arc, where journeys wend.
Each hue a promise, bright and true,
In cosmic realms, where dreams break through.

From distant stars, the light cascades,
Through shimmering fields where wonder wades.
Romantic whispers in the stellar haze,
Invite us forth to endless praise.

On feathered wings, we soar so high,
Chasing the streaks 'neath the azure sky.
With laughter ringing, the heart in flight,
In cosmic dance, we find our light.

As dawn awakens, the colors bloom,
From violet dusk to gold's perfume.
A symphony woven in radiant beams,
In every pulse, the universe dreams.

So come, dear soul, let wonder guide,
Through rainbows bright, we shall confide.
For in the ether, magic sways,
And life becomes a vivid haze.

Echoes of Silk Beneath Starlit Skies

In twilight's hush, the fabric sighs,
Of silk that flutters 'neath starlit skies.
With every thread, a story spun,
Of loves once lost and battles won.

Beneath the glow of distant stars,
The night reveals its hidden scars.
Each echo whispers of what's gone,
Yet in the dark, new dreams are drawn.

With silken whispers, shadows play,
Casting their nets in the soft decay.
In velvet realms where silence reigns,
The heart beats softly, love remains.

The galaxies twirl in cosmic dance,
While weaves of fate weave circumstance.
In threads of fate, each moment glows,
As starlit time in silence flows.

So draw your cloak and breathe the night,
For dreams may linger in gentle light.
In echoes soft, let magic rise,
To twine with silk 'neath starlit skies.

The Tapestry of Colors and Celestial Beings

In realms where colors burst and play,
A tapestry unfolds each day.
With threads of joy and threads of fear,
Celestial beings linger near.

The sun, a brush, paints skies aglow,
With hues of love, as soft winds blow.
While stars embroider the night so dark,
In whirls of light, they leave a mark.

From every petal, from every sigh,
A song of life begins to fly.
Where wonders bloom and moments weave,
We find the magic we believe.

The moonlight dances on silver streams,
Awakening our long-held dreams.
In whispered tones, the cosmos sings,
Of timeless tales and hidden things.

So gaze upon this wondrous art,
The tapestry holds each beating heart.
With colors bright and spirits bold,
We share our stories, waiting to be told.

Beyond the Veil: A Journey Through Hued Mysteries

In shadows deep, where secrets dwell,
Colors weave a whispered spell.
Each hue a tale, a story spun,
Beneath the moon, the world is won.

With every brush, the night unfurls,
A tapestry of dreamlike swirls.
Emerald stars and sapphire skies,
In twilight's gaze, the magic lies.

Through veils of mist, the wanderers roam,
In search of lights that lead them home.
Crimson calls from the forest's heart,
A longing deep that won't depart.

With each new shade, the spirit stirs,
In the silence, the cosmos purrs.
Underneath the world's great dome,
A symphony of hues, a soul's poem.

Beyond the veil, where dreams awake,
A vibrant path for all to take.
Together we dance in the painted night,
As stars descend, in pure delight.

Whispers of Dusk in Gilded Dreams

At dusk's embrace, the shadows play,
Golden glimmers fade to gray.
The air is thick with secrets old,
Sweet stories waiting to be told.

With every breath, a wish is cast,
In drifting winds, the moments pass.
Gilded dreams on the canvas flow,
As twilight's fire begins to glow.

The whispers soft as stars ignite,
Stitching warmth into the night.
A lullaby of hues that blend,
A signal that this time won't end.

In softest silence, hearts align,
With fleeting glimpses, worlds entwine.
We trace the paths of fading light,
In gilded dreams, we take our flight.

So let us drift on evening's breeze,
In whispered tones beneath the trees.
For dusk, with all its painted schemes,
Reveals a world of gilded dreams.

Celestial Hues and Enchanted Glimmers

From heaven's vault, the colors pour,
Celestial hues, forevermore.
In twilight's grace, the stardust streams,
A canvas bright, where wonder gleams.

The azure night unveils its charm,
While silver dreams entwine and swarm.
Each glimmer sparkles, soft and pure,
In magic's grasp, our hearts endure.

As constellations weave their tale,
We dance beneath their luminous trail.
Emerald sparks leap from the sky,
A radiant pulse that will not die.

Sapphire oceans, amethyst skies,
Within their depths, our spirits rise.
In every hue, an echo plays,
A symphony of night's embrace.

We wander through this vibrant sight,
In celestial hues, we find our light.
With enchanted glimmers by our side,
We sail through dreams on night's tide.

A Palette of Illusions at Twilight's Edge

At twilight's edge, illusions bloom,
A canvas drawn in soft perfume.
Brushstrokes blend from dusk till dawn,
Painting whispers, twilight's song.

The palette spills with shades of hope,
In twilight's grasp, we learn to cope.
Violet echoes and marigold sighs,
A world reborn beneath changing skies.

Hues of longing flow and dance,
In every glance, a fleeting chance.
Cosmic mysteries yet untold,
Unravel truths both bright and bold.

We chase the night, where shadows creep,
Among the dreams we long to keep.
In every color, a story lies,
A whispered promise as daylight dies.

A palette rich with love and fear,
Each stroke of fate draws us near.
At twilight's edge, we find our voice,
In the art of night, we softly rejoice.

So let the brush of time create,
A world where illusions celebrate.
In hues of dusk, we craft our home,
As twilight calls, we are not alone.

Secrets Hidden in Fragments of Twilight

When shadows fall and whispers breathe,
The secrets stir beneath the leaves.
In twilight's grip, the world transforms,
Unveiling truths in hidden forms.

A flicker here, a shimmer there,
The magic dances through the air.
In fragments caught by fading light,
The heart knows well what hides from sight.

Among the stars, the stories gleam,
Each one a thread of a forgotten dream.
In twilight's hush, the secrets weave,
A tapestry that none perceive.

The nightingale sings softly low,
As moonlit paths begin to glow.
Within each glance, a mystery waits,
Unlocking softly the ancient gates.

So listen close, and you may find,
The echoes left by the unseen kind.
For in the dusk, where shadows hide,
Lie secrets steeped in starry pride.

The Kaleidoscope of Wonders Beyond the Veil

Beyond the veil, where spirits play,
A kaleidoscope lights the way.
With hues that twist and turn with grace,
Revealing worlds in every space.

Each color sings a different tune,
A serenade of stars and moon.
Within the dance of shapes and light,
Mysteries bloom in sheer delight.

With every blink, a tale unfurls,
Spinning dreams of distant worlds.
In vibrant shades, they intertwine,
Whispering secrets, yours and mine.

As echoes fade with each new glance,
The wonders weave a fleeting dance.
In this embrace of light's delight,
We find our paths in the starry night.

So seize the magic, hold it near,
For worlds await, both far and near.
In colors bright, beyond the veil,
The spirit sings of every tale.

Echoing Colors in the Garden of Secrets

In gardens rich with whispered hues,
Echoing colors weave their muse.
Each petal holds a tale untold,
Of secrets buried, brave and bold.

The rustling leaves, a gentle sigh,
As dreams escape into the sky.
With every breeze, the truths emerge,
In swirling patterns, they converge.

Watch closely now, the shadows dance,
In soft embrace, they take a chance.
With whispered laughs, the secrets grow,
In every heart, a radiant glow.

The twilight blooms, a canvas rare,
As starlit stories fill the air.
In every corner, magic stirs,
In gardens lush where love occurs.

So stroll within this sacred space,
Where colors sing and time finds grace.
In echoing shades, the heart will find,
The garden holds the dreams entwined.

Lush Tones of the Enigmatic Horizon

Upon the horizon, colors swell,
In lush tones where the silence dwells.
A canvas spread with every dream,
Embracing the night with a brilliant gleam.

As dusk descends, the world ignites,
With shades that whisper, beckon, fright.
From rich mahogany to softest jade,
An enigmatic dance is lovingly laid.

The stars emerge, a radiant choir,
Singing softly of wishes dire.
In each shimmer, a story lingers,
Caught in the fold of time's deft fingers.

With every breath, the horizon sighs,
Unraveling truths beneath the skies.
The lush tones blend, an artist's brush,
Creating magic within the hush.

So gaze upon this wondrous sight,
Where shadows wane and dreams take flight.
In every hue, in every arc,
The soul finds peace in the lingering spark.

Colors of Lullabies in the Realm of Starlight

In the hush of night, the colors glow,
Whispers of dreams in a gentle flow.
Crimson and azure, a soft embrace,
Painting the skies, a starlit space.

Golden light dances on silver beams,
Where lullabies weave through moonlit dreams.
Indigo shadows, soft as a sigh,
Bathe the world as the night drifts by.

Emerald echoes in twilight's lull,
Create a canvas, mysterious and dull.
Each shade, a secret, softly spoken,
In the realm where the stars are woken.

Violet whispers call through the dark,
As the nightingale sings out her spark.
Crimson cascades in a velvet stream,
Guiding the wanderers, lost in their dream.

Under the spell where shadows convene,
The colors of lullabies twinkle serene.
In the starlit realm where wishes take flight,
All hearts are cradled in the arms of night.

Enigmatic Hues Beneath the Enchanted Arch

Beneath the arch where mysteries blend,
Ember and sapphire together transcend.
Flickering lanterns in shades so bold,
Tell tales of wonders, secrets unfold.

A cascade of amethyst drapes the ground,
Where dreams and wishes are quietly found.
Cerulean breezes whisper of lore,
Caressing the night, forevermore.

Beryl moonlight, delicate and bright,
Leads wandering souls through the tapestry of night.
With each step taken, the shadows will play,
In hues that dance softly, guiding the way.

Rustling leaves shout in colors unseen,
An aurora of echoes, enchanting and keen.
With every heartbeat, the archway will sway,
As night falls sweetly, ushering day.

In the realm of whispers, the colors sing,
Creating a tapestry, ephemeral and bling.
Enigmatic hues that under stars swim,
Welcoming dreamers, hearts ready to brim.

The Chromatic Embrace of Otherworldly Echoes

In the realm of echoes, colors unfurl,
Through valleys of twilight and stardust pearl.
A tapestry woven by galactic hands,
Weaving the whispers of magical lands.

Scarlet sunsets kiss the edges of night,
Painting the heavens with glowing light.
Emerald forests glimmer with grace,
While moonbeams sparkle, a silvery lace.

The echoes carry memories untold,
In hues of the heart, vibrant and bold.
Gold textures flutter on the wings of dreams,
Beneath the starlight, everything gleams.

With every heartbeat, the world twirls around,
In chromatic embraces, serenity found.
Curious spirits entwined in the glow,
Of otherworldly echoes, soft and slow.

As the dawn approaches, colors shift anew,
Bringing the warmth of a sky so blue.
Each hue a promise, each echo a song,
In this wondrous ballet, where we all belong.

Illumination of Fantasia in a Dreamlike Landscape

In the warmth of dawn, colors start to bloom,
Awakening dreams through the fragrant room.
A symphony crafted from radiant light,
Where the fantastical dances in pure delight.

Emerging from shadows, the pastels arise,
Illuminating the path where wonder lies.
Lavender dreams brush the edges of time,
In landscapes of whimsy, so vivid, sublime.

Glistening rivers, with golden flow,
Reflect every wish that the heart longs to know.
Amber skies wrap the world in a hug,
Embracing the magic like a warm, soft rug.

In the flicker of fireflies, a symphony sings,
In each twinkling light, hope's gentle wings.
Chasing the echoes of laughter and grace,
Within the lush dreams of this wondrous space.

So wander through color, let the heart feel,
In this dreamlike landscape, let magic be real.
Illumination dances in graceful array,
As dreams intertwine in the light of the day.

Spectrum of Dreams on Forgotten Paths

In the hush of twilight's veil,
Where shadows dance and secrets sail,
Whispers of wishes float on air,
Through forgotten paths, we dream and dare.

Colors bleed in twilight's glow,
Painting dreams in vibrant flow,
Every step on this winding trail,
Leads to stories where hearts prevail.

Silent echoes of laughter ring,
As memory's chimes gently sing,
With each footfall, a spark ignites,
Illuminating our starry nights.

In the realm where hopes reside,
A universe of dreams inside,
We chase the glimmers, bold and bright,
Born from the depths of endless night.

Through paths of enchantment, we roam wide,
With stardust guiding, dreams as our guide,
In the spectrum where wishes blend,
A tapestry of journey without end.

The Incandescent Canvas of Mythic Journeys

Upon the canvas, stories blend,
With strokes of fate, the colors send,
Brush against the edges of time,
Where myth and magic in rhythm rhyme.

Each tale a star, each journey bright,
Casting shadows, igniting light,
In words that dance like flames and dreams,
We find our paths in vivid themes.

From distant realms to shores unknown,
We chase the echoes of the lone,
In every whisper, worlds unfold,
With secrets rich and tales retold.

The palette swirls with hopes and fears,
As laughter mingles with falling tears,
We traverse through the ancient lore,
In the incandescent glow, we soar.

So paint your story, bold and true,
In vibrant hues, let dreams imbue,
For in this canvas, life may rise,
To fill the world with wonder's guise.

Chromatic Whispers in the Twilight Breeze

In the twilight's soft embrace,
Whispers echo, shadows trace,
Colors twirl on gentle air,
With secrets we are bound to share.

Every breeze a tale untold,
In chromatic hues of gold,
We gather dreams like drifting leaves,
In time's embrace, our heart believes.

A tapestry of dusk and dawn,
Where hopes are spun and fears withdrawn,
We chase the colors of the light,
In whispers wrapped, our spirits take flight.

Each moment holds a precious spark,
In twilight's glow, we leave our mark,
With laughter painting skies so wide,
In chromatic whirls, we find our guide.

So let us dance in colors bright,
As whispers merge with fading light,
For in the twilight's tender breeze,
We weave our dreams among the trees.

Vivid Recollections in the Field of Stardust

In the field where stardust gleams,
Memories spin like whispered dreams,
Each twinkle holds a tale unique,
In the silence, our spirits speak.

Vivid colors splash the skies,
With every glance, a world replies,
In the shimmer of the night's embrace,
Recollections dance in boundless space.

From laughter shared to tears of grace,
Each moment captured in time's warm face,
In the field of dreams, we chase the past,
With stardust trails that ever last.

Embrace the sparkle, hold it near,
In the echoes of the heart's frontier,
For vivid memories come alive,
In stardust fields, our dreams revive.

So let us wander, hand in hand,
Through realms of memory, bright and grand,
In every star, our stories lie,
In the field of stardust, we will fly.

Enchanted Contrasts in a Ethereal Sea

In a sea where moonlight plays,
Waves whisper secrets of the night.
Shadows dance in silken rays,
Where dreams take flight in pure delight.

Colors blend in twilight's mist,
Emerald greens and sapphire blues.
A hidden world that won't be missed,
Wrapped in magic's gentle hues.

Mermaids sing in liquid gold,
Their voices weave through ocean's lore.
Every tale a thrill retold,
Vowing to keep you wanting more.

A ship sails on, with sails aglow,
Guided by the stars' embrace.
In this realm where wonders flow,
Adventure finds its rightful place.

Ethereal tunes light up the tide,
With every swell, the heart ignites.
A contrast where fears subside,
In this enchanted sea of nights.

The Allure of Color in Forgotten Realms

In a land where colors fade,
Once vibrant hues now hushed with time.
Whispers of a memory made,
As shadows dance in muted rhyme.

Wonders lost, yet stories bloom,
In corners where the old trees sigh.
Leaving only a scent of gloom,
Echoes of laughter passing by.

Rivers twist through emerald glades,
Crimson flowers brave the strife.
Each petal spins a tale that wades,
Through the threads of fading life.

A castle stands with walls of mist,
Painted stories, fading fast.
In every corner, dreams still twist,
Holding on to glories past.

Yet in the dark, a spark ignites,
Reminding souls of what was real.
Colors dance in moonlit nights,
As forgotten realms begin to heal.

Shaded Memories upon Luminescent Paths

In the woods where silence breathes,
Footsteps falter on quiet ground.
Every leaf a tale that weaves,
Through the memories, sweetly found.

Misty glows lead hearts astray,
Guiding lost souls through the dark.
Shadows shelter dreams at play,
While whispers dance in the park.

Moonlit trails paint stories bright,
Underneath the ancient trees.
Past secrets come alive at night,
Carried softly by the breeze.

Glimmers chase away the gloom,
As echoes of laughter tread near.
Every corner, a blossomed bloom,
Holding tightly to yesteryear.

With each step, the shadows blend,
Past and present tightly twine.
Upon the paths where memories mend,
Luminescent signs align.

The Glow of Magic in the Heart of Night

In the heart of midnight's veil,
Magic stirs in shadows deep.
When silence casts its gentle tale,
And stars awaken from their sleep.

Bright stardust falls like silver rain,
Crowning dreams with twinkling light.
In every drop, the joy and pain,
A dance unfolding in the night.

From ancient crypts where whispers dwell,
The glow of magic starts to rise.
Casting spells that weave their spell,
A tapestry beneath dark skies.

With every twist, the air ignites,
Filling hearts with wonder's spark.
In this realm of whispered sights,
Secrets breathe beneath the dark.

Awake, arise, and chase the glow,
Let the moonlight guide your way.
In the heart of magic's flow,
Night reveals what dreams can sway.

www.ingramcontent.com/pod-product-compliance
Ingram Content Group UK Ltd.
Pitfield, Milton Keynes, MK11 3LW, UK
UKHW021439290125
4349UKWH00039B/539

9 781805 637455